Mathematical Merry-go-round

Whole class oral activities to enhance the curriculum

Vivien Lucas

 Tarquin

Mathematical Merry-go-round

The essential point about these activities, is that they take place instantly and in 'real time', as computer experts call it. As each question is read out, the pupils are required to respond in a variety of different ways. Sometimes they have to hold up a card or a whiteboard, sometimes they have to answer in turn and sometimes they have to fill in a simple chart or table.

What is required is a speedy response and an active participation by everyone in the class. Everything is intended to be under the direct control and supervision of the teacher and as a result a considerable atmosphere of fun, enthusiasm and enjoyment can be generated.

Calculators are not required for any of the activities and indeed many of the questions are deliberately made to be relatively easy. It is the principle and the idea which is being reinforced added to the fun of active participation. You may well find that some of the activities can also be used as good lesson starters. They get everyone focussed and thinking on a suitable topic straight away. The aim throughout all these activities is to create a lively, enjoyable atmosphere where everyone becomes alert and involved.

Why use multiple choice activities?

Pupils who often struggle with the written side of mathematics get a chance to shine in this kind of activity. Where the pupils have to choose between various possible answers and respond by holding up a lettered card, there is no need for writing or explaining. Timid pupils who are reluctant to put up their hands to give a detailed answer may often be perfectly happy to hold up simple answer card with an A, B, C, or D on it.

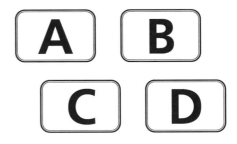

Setting up the activities

The activities really fall into two main categories: those where pupils all work out their answers at the same time and those where pupils have to answer in turn. The former can be well be played with the pupils sitting at their usual places, but the latter are best played with the pupils seated or standing in a circle or horseshoe arrangement around the outside of the room. It greatly helps to maintain the speed and order of response if it is quite clear whose turn is next. For activity 11, the memory game, the fact that everyone is facing inwards provides a powerful aid to the memories as the game approaches its later stages.

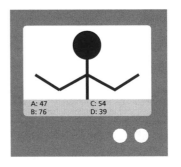

Adapting to curriculum needs

The questions included in this book are all based on the normal curriculum but once any particular game idea has been tested and proved to work then it becomes a simple matter to construct further sets of questions on any part of the curriculum which you feel needs attention. Often blank masters and worksheets have been provided in order to make it easier to prepare your own, personally-tuned questions for any particular class.

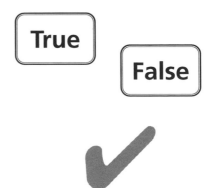

Special occasions

Some of these activities can be used and adapted for special maths days or maths clubs which take place outside normal hours. Such activities as these are perceived to be less formal and more like a game and so for these special situations they can offer just what is needed.

Making the photocopies

Most of the A4 photocopy masters of the data or the alternatives can be simply copied and handed out in the normal way. However, to save space in this book some are expected to be enlarged by up to 141%. In this way an A5 half-page becomes a full A4 page. This is particularly useful when making the response cards with the letters A, B, C, D and 'True' & 'False'. There are strong advantages from an organisational point of view if those cards are photocopied on to card of different colours. Since they can be used for different activities and a various times during the school year, it might be a good idea to laminate the A4 sheets before cutting them up into the individual sets of cards. Often one sheet will make four of these cards.

141%

What is required?

For each of the sixteen activities there is a statement to remind you what is needed for yourself and what needs to be prepared for each of the pupils. There is also a suggestion of the procedure to be followed. Of course, once you have got the idea working well it will not be difficult to construct more examples or to vary the rules and the approach.

Incentives

Some of the games have a scoring system and some produce an absolute winner. On some occasions it might be a good idea to have some small prizes, sweets or merit points.

Active participation is guaranteed!

Mathematical Millionaire

This activity, loosely based on the television game 'Who Wants to be a Millionaire?', has fifteen questions to mirror the fifteen steps on the way to a prize of one million. It is a very good activity for revising certain topics, especially those where pupils find it difficult to remember precisely what the rules are.

Speed is of the essence and it is not a good idea for the questions to be too difficult. Set A with its testing of algebraic substitution is a particularly good one to start with.

What does each pupil require?
Four cards with the letters A, B, C, D preferably in different colours
An 'alternatives' answer sheet.

What does the teacher require?
A set of questions and their answers
A list of the names of the pupils taking part

Procedure:
Read out a question and ask them to enter it into the space on their 'alternatives' sheet. Allow about 10 seconds and then say 'show'. At this point everyone should hold up one of the four cards A, B, C, D to indicate the answer.

It is a good idea to have a list of the names in the class and mark down just those who got it wrong. The advantage of the different colours for different answers will be apparent here.

Continue reading out one question at a time all the way up to 15. Everyone who has not given a single wrong answer is then a 'mathematical millionaire'.

A variation that could be used is to divide the class into two teams. Ideally each team should sit in a circle. After each question the members of each team show their chosen answers to the team leader who then decides which choice will be the team's answer. The job of team leader moves round the circle after each question. The teams should be asked alternately to give their teams answer first. The team scores can then be displayed on the board.

The form for the fourth set has been left blank so that you can easily construct quizzes exactly tuned to your own class and the topic needing revision.

Set A: Algebra substitution and negative numbers

$p = 3, q = -4, r = 5, s = -6$

1.	$p - q + r + s$	C	6
2.	$4p + 2q + 3r$	B	19
3.	$pr - qs$	D	-9
4.	$p^2 + s^2$	A	45
5.	$p^2 + q^2 - r^2$	B	0
6.	$2p^2 + 2q^2$	D	50
7.	$3(q + r)^2$	C	3
8.	$(5p + 3q)^2$	D	9
9.	qrs	D	120
10.	$6p - qr$	A	38
11.	$rs \div p$	C	-10
12.	$p^2q - pq^2$	B	12
13.	$r^2 + s^2 \div p^2$	D	29
14.	$(2s)^2 - 2s^2$	A	72
15.	$8r^2 - (5q)^2$	C	-200

Set B The Properties of circles

1.	Area of a circle of radius 8cm.	C	64π cm²
2.	Circumference of a circle of diameter 10cm	B	10π cm
3.	Area of a circle of diameter 12cm.	D	36π cm²
4.	Circumference of a circle of radius 7cm.	B	14π cm
5.	Area of a semicircle of radius 4cm.	A	8π cm²
6.	Perimeter of a semicircle of diameter 8cm.	C	$(4\pi + 8)$cm
7.	Area of a quarter circle of diameter 16cm.	D	16π cm²
8.	Perimeter of a quarter circle of radius 2cm.	B	$(\pi + 4)$cm
9.	Area of biggest circle inside a 6cm square	C	9π cm²
10.	Diameter of a circle of circumference 50cm.	A	$50/\pi$ cm
11.	Radius of a circle of area 80cm².	D	$\sqrt{(80/\pi)}$ cm
12.	Radius of a circle of circumference 64cm.	B	$32/\pi$ cm
13.	Diameter of a circle where the number of cm in the circumference equals twice the number of cm² in the area.	D	2 cm
14.	Radius of a circle where the number of cm² in the area equals eight times the number of cm in the circumference.	C	16 cm
15.	Diameter of a circle of area 120cm².	A	$\sqrt{(480/\pi)}$cm

---

Set C: Decimal places

1.	0.3 x 0 2	B	0.06
2.	0.3 x 0.4	C	0.12
3.	0.5 x 0.01	A	0.005
4.	0.06 x 0.03	C	0.0018
5.	0.05 x 0.04	D	0.002
6.	1.01 x 0.03	C	0.0303
7.	0.005 x 0.06	A	0.0003
8.	0.04²	C	0.0016
9.	0.0028 ÷ 4	D	0.0007
10.	0.00054 ÷ 6	A	0.00009
11.	0.24 ÷ 0.8	D	0.3
12.	0.0015 ÷ 0.03	C	0.05
13.	0.004 ÷ 0.08	C	0.05
14.	0.2 x 0.6 ÷ 0.4	B	0.3
15.	0.05 x 0.04 ÷ 0.02	C	0.1

If someone asks, the 15 steps on the way to a million in the TV show are £100, £200, £300, £500, £1 000, £2 000, £4 000, £8 000, £16 000, £32 000, £64 000, £125 000, £250 000, £500 000, and £1 000 000.

Mathematical Millionaire

Set A: Algebra, Substitution and Negative Numbers

p = 3, q = -4, r = 5, s = -6

Choices

Questions		A	B	C	D
1		-2	10	6	18
2		35	19	5	11
3		-3	9	-5	-9
4		45	-27	18	-6
5		-32	0	50	4
6		-14	100	-28	50
7		54	243	3	6
8		4	-9	38	9
9		-90	-120	90	120
10		38	70	110	93
11		10	8	-10	-8
12		48	12	-12	0
13		$6\frac{7}{9}$	$-1\frac{2}{9}$	12	29
14		72	0	-48	216
15		200	1200	-200	120

Mathematical Merry-go-round - Mathematical Millionaire

Set B: The Properties of circles

Choices

Questions		A	B	C	D
1	cm^2	8π	16π	64π	56π
2	cm	5π	10π	20π	25π
3	cm^2	6π	72π	144π	36π
4	cm	7π	14π	49π	28π
5	cm^2	8π	4π	2π	16π
6	cm	$8\pi + 8$	$4\pi + 4$	$4\pi + 8$	$8\pi + 4$
7	cm^2	64π	48π	32π	16π
8	cm	$\pi + 2$	$\pi + 4$	$2\pi + 2$	$4\pi + 4$
9	cm^2	3π	6π	9π	36π
10	cm	$\frac{50}{\pi}$	$\frac{25}{\pi}$	$\frac{\pi}{50}$	$\frac{100}{\pi}$
11	cm	$\frac{80}{\pi}$	$\sqrt{\left(\frac{160}{\pi}\right)}$	$\sqrt{\left(\frac{40}{\pi}\right)}$	$\sqrt{\left(\frac{80}{\pi}\right)}$
12	cm	$\frac{64}{\pi}$	$\frac{32}{\pi}$	$\frac{128}{\pi}$	$\frac{\pi}{32}$
13	cm	$\frac{1}{2}$	4	1	2
14	cm	2	4	16	8
15	cm	$\sqrt{\left(\frac{480}{\pi}\right)}$	$\sqrt{\left(\frac{120}{\pi}\right)}$	$\sqrt{\left(\frac{240}{\pi}\right)}$	$\frac{60}{\pi}$

Mathematical Merry-go-round - Mathematical Millionaire

Mathematical Millionaire

Set C: Decimal Places

	Questions	Choices			
		A	**B**	**C**	**D**
1		0.6	0.06	0.006	0.0006
2		0.0012	0.0012	0.12	1.2
3		0.005	0.05	0.5	0.0005
4		0.18	0.018	0.0018	0.00018
5		0.2	0.02	0.0002	0.002
6		3.03	0.303	0.0303	0.00303
7		0.0003	0.003	0.03	0.3
8		0.16	0.08	0.0016	0.0008
9		0.7	0.07	0.007	0.0007
10		0.00009	0.0009	0.009	0.09
11		3	0.03	0.003	0.3
12		5	0.5	0.05	0.005
13		5	0.5	0.05	0.005
14		0.003	0.3	0.03	3
15		10	1	0.1	0.01

Blank Set

	Questions	Choices			
		A	**B**	**C**	**D**
1					
2					
3					
4					
5					
6					
7					
8					
9					
10					
11					
12					
13					
14					
15					

Mathematical Millionaire

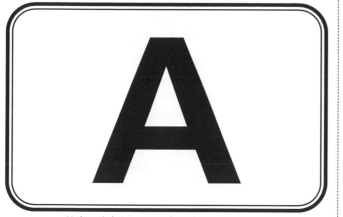

Mathematical Merry-go-round - Mathematical Millionaire

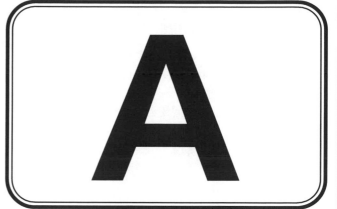

Mathematical Merry-go-round - Mathematical Millionaire

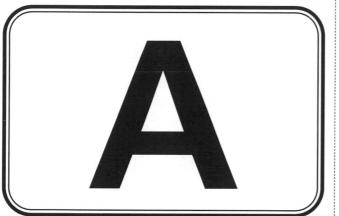

Mathematical Merry-go-round - Mathematical Millionaire

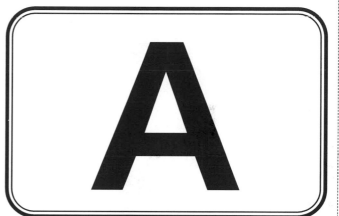

Mathematical Merry-go-round - Mathematical Millionaire

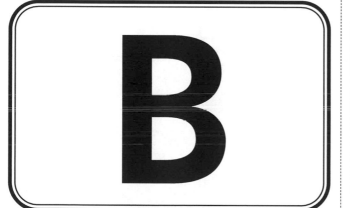

Mathematical Merry-go-round - Mathematical Millionaire

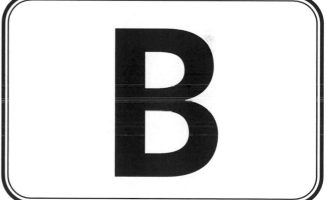

Mathematical Merry-go-round - Mathematical Millionaire

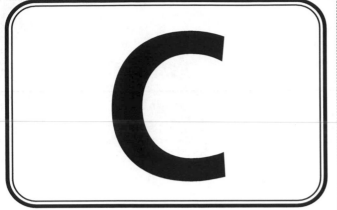

Mathematical Merry-go-round - Mathematical Millionaire

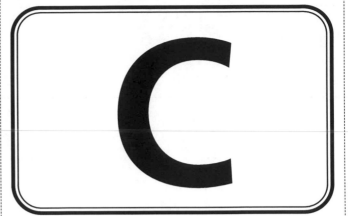

Mathematical Merry-go-round - Mathematical Millionaire

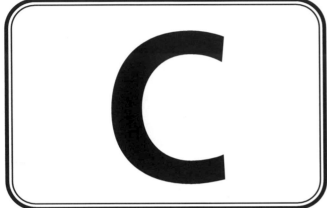

Mathematical Merry-go-round - Mathematical Millionaire

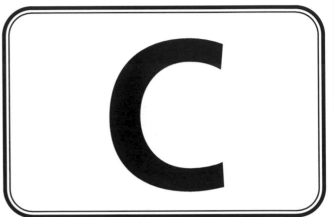

Mathematical Merry-go-round - Mathematical Millionaire

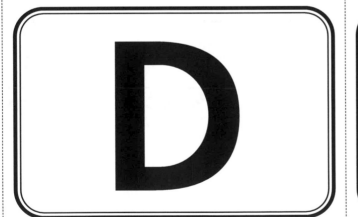

Mathematical Merry-go-round - Mathematical Millionaire

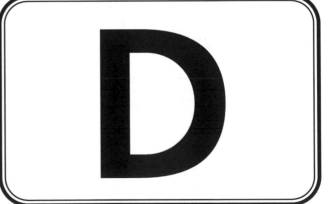

Mathematical Merry-go-round - Mathematical Millionaire

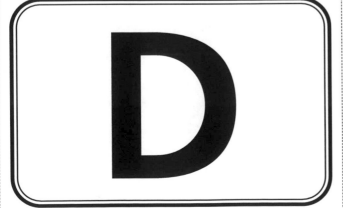

Mathematical Merry-go-round - Mathematical Millionaire

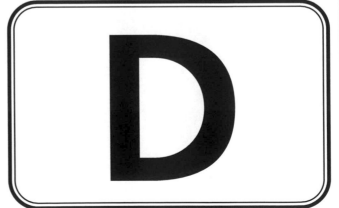

Mathematical Merry-go-round - Mathematical Millionaire

Odd One Out

This can be a fun activity for a suitable class and is a simple test of memory and concentration as well as the topic under practice or revision. The level of difficulty of the two examples given below is not high and indeed cannot be so, because for the students there is a real difficulty in retaining all four sums in their minds while doing the calculations which will eliminate three of them.

What does each pupil require?
A set of A, B, C, D cards from pages 7 and 8.

What does the teacher require?
Sets of four questions where three of them are equivalent and the fourth has an answer which is very close to the others. It should not be possible to make a sensible guess at the right answer purely on the grounds of size.

(Pupils could be given paper for working out but they should not be allowed to use calculators.)

Procedure:
The teacher reads out the four alternative answers in a suitably measured way. The class members then have to hold up the letter that matches the answer that differs from the other three. It is good idea to say something like 'now' after leaving a few seconds for thought so that all the class show their cards at the same time.

It is useful to have a list of all the names in the class and mark down just those who got it wrong. Answer cards in different colours will make this process much easier.

Set A: Arithmetic

	A	B	C	D	✓
1	4 x 6	3 x 8	$\frac{1}{2}$ of 48	15 + 8	D
2	3 x 12	16 x 2	9 x 4	6^2	B
3	8 + 8	20 - 4	2 x 9	80 ÷ 5	C
4	5^2	$\frac{1}{4}$ of 100	32 - 7	19 + 7	D
5	39 + 5	6 x 7	$\frac{1}{2}$ of 84	14 x 3	A
6	8 x 8	15 x 4	3 x 20	$8^2 - 2^2$	A
7	7 x 8	9 x 6	$\frac{1}{2}$ of 112	14 x 4	B
8	9 x 8	6 x 12	18 x 4	38 x 2	D
9	10 x 5	$7^2 + 1^2$	25 x 3	$\frac{1}{5}$ of 250	C
10	12 x 7	2 x 42	100 - 26	6 x 14	C
11	9 x 9	$\frac{1}{3}$ of 246	3^4	27 x 3	B
12	5 x 15	$\frac{1}{2}$ of 150	3 x 25	110 - 45	D
13	88 + 6	$10^2 - 2^2$	12 x 8	6 x 16	A
14	120 - 3^2	30 + 81	37 x 3	57 x 2	D
15	8 x 18	35 x 4	9 x 16	3 x 48	B

Set B: Equivalent fractions

	A	B	C	D	✓
1	$\frac{2}{4}$	$\frac{4}{8}$	$\frac{14}{26}$	$\frac{6}{12}$	C
2	$\frac{7}{24}$	$\frac{1}{4}$	$\frac{3}{12}$	$\frac{4}{16}$	A
3	$\frac{6}{18}$	$\frac{8}{21}$	$\frac{1}{3}$	$\frac{5}{15}$	B
4	$\frac{4}{10}$	$\frac{9}{20}$	$\frac{12}{30}$	$\frac{2}{5}$	B
5	$\frac{1}{6}$	$\frac{3}{18}$	$\frac{5}{30}$	$\frac{8}{54}$	D
6	$\frac{16}{21}$	$\frac{2}{3}$	$\frac{16}{24}$	$\frac{22}{33}$	A
7	$\frac{75}{100}$	$\frac{21}{24}$	$\frac{3}{4}$	$\frac{12}{16}$	B
8	$\frac{24}{40}$	$\frac{3}{5}$	$\frac{27}{35}$	$\frac{21}{35}$	C
9	$\frac{40}{56}$	$\frac{5}{6}$	$\frac{15}{18}$	$\frac{55}{66}$	A
10	$\frac{7}{10}$	$\frac{21}{30}$	$\frac{72}{90}$	$\frac{42}{60}$	C
11	$\frac{15}{40}$	$\frac{36}{96}$	$\frac{21}{54}$	$\frac{3}{8}$	C
12	$\frac{12}{21}$	$\frac{4}{7}$	$\frac{28}{49}$	$\frac{8}{15}$	D
13	$\frac{24}{30}$	$\frac{32}{45}$	$\frac{4}{5}$	$\frac{80}{100}$	A
14	$\frac{5}{8}$	$\frac{60}{100}$	$\frac{25}{40}$	$\frac{125}{200}$	B
15	$\frac{21}{27}$	$\frac{175}{225}$	$\frac{7}{9}$	$\frac{164}{216}$	D

Coordinate Words

This activity is a way of both revising the accurate reading of coordinates and of reinforcing mathematical vocabulary. All 26 letters of the alphabet have been placed at whole-number coordinates on both sides of both axes. They have also been positioned in a rather symmetrical way to encourage accurate reading and to help make certain that the differences between (-3,2), (-2,3), (3,-2) and (2,-3), for instance, are clearly appreciated.

What does each pupil require?
A photocopy of the diagram of the letters of the alphabet on the two alternative coordinate grids.

What does the teacher require?
A set of about ten coordinate questions leading to suitable words from the mathematical vocabulary, chosen for the class or topic in question.

Procedure:
Read out sets of coordinates in a suitable measured way and ask the pupils to write down the words that appear. It is probably best to wait until all ten questions in a set have been answered before comparing or marking.

As a follow-up, why not ask for definitions of each of the answers in the least possible number of words?

QUESTIONS SET A
1. (-3,2) (-3,-2) (2,3) (-1,2) = CUBE
2. (-1,1) (-3,1) (3,-1) (-1,2) = KITE
3. (-2,3) (1,-2) (-3,1) (2,-1)
4. (-2,3) (3,1) (2,2) (1,1) (-1,2)
5. (1,-1) (-2,3) (-2,2) (-3,1) (-3,-2) (2,-1)
6. (-3,2) (-3,1) (1,-1) (-3,2) (1,1) (-1,2)
7. (2,-1) (-1,-1) (-3,-2) (-2,3) (1,-1) (-1,2)
8. (-3,-1) (2,3) (3,-1) (-3,-2) (2,-1) (-1,2)
9. (1,-1) (-1,2) (1,2) (1,1) (-1,2) (1,-2)
10. (2,-1) (-2,-1) (3,2) (-1,2) (1,-1) (-1,2)

ANSWERS SET A
1. CUBE
2. KITE
3. AXIS
4. ANGLE
5. RADIUS
6. CIRCLE
7. SQUARE
8. OBTUSE
9. REFLEX
10. SPHERE

QUESTIONS SET B
1. (0,4) (-2,0) (1,1) (4,4)
2. (2,4) (-4,4) (3,-1) (-4,4)
3. (0,-4) (4,4) (-1,-1) (-2,0)
4. (-4,4) (0,4) (-2,-2) (3,-1) (4,4)
5. (2,0) (-1,-1) (3,3) (1,-1) (-1,1)
6. (-1,3) (-1,-1) (-4,4) (2,0) (1,3)
7. (-3,3) (-4,4) (0,4) (3,-1) (-2,0) (-1-1)
8. (1,-1) (-4,4) (-1,1) (2,0) (2,2) (4,4)
9. (0,4) (-2,0) (1,1) (0,-2) (4,4) (-1,-3)
10. (0,-2) (-2,0) (2,2) (-2,-2) (-1,1) (4,4)

ANSWERS SET B
1. CONE
2. DATA
3. ZERO
4. ACUTE
5. PRISM
6. GRAPH
7. FACTOR
8. SAMPLE
9. CONVEX
10. VOLUME

It is not difficult to construct more sets of questions and words if they are required for either or both grid systems. You can also get the pupils to prepare words for the rest of the class to try. You need to specify what words are suitable otherwise you get words like MANUNITED!

Alphabet using Set A Coordinates			
A = (-2,3)	B = (2,3)	C = (-3,2)	D = (-2,2)
E = (-1,2)	F = (1,2)	G = (2,2)	H = (3,2)
I = (-3,1)	J = (-2,1)	K = (-1,1)	L = (1,1)
M = (2,1)	N = (3,1)	O = (-3,-1)	P = (-2,-1)
Q = (-1,-1)	R = (1,-1)	S = (2,-1)	T = (3,-1)
U = (-3,-2)	V = (-2,-2)	W = (-1,-2)	X = (1,-2)
Y = (2,-2)	Z = (3,-2)		

Alphabet using Set B Coordinates			
A = (-4,4)	B = (-2,4)	C = (0,4)	D = (2,4)
E = (4,4)	F = (-3,3)	G = (-1,3)	H = (1,3)
I = (3,3)	J = (-2,2)	K = (0,2)	L = (2,2)
M = (-1,1)	N = (1,1)	O = (-2,0)	P = (2,0)
Q = (-3,-1)	R = (-1,-1)	S = (1,-1)	T = (3,-1)
U = (-2,-2)	V = (0,-2)	W = (2,-2)	X = (-1,-3)
Y = (1,-3)	Z = (0,-4)		

Coordinate Words

Set A

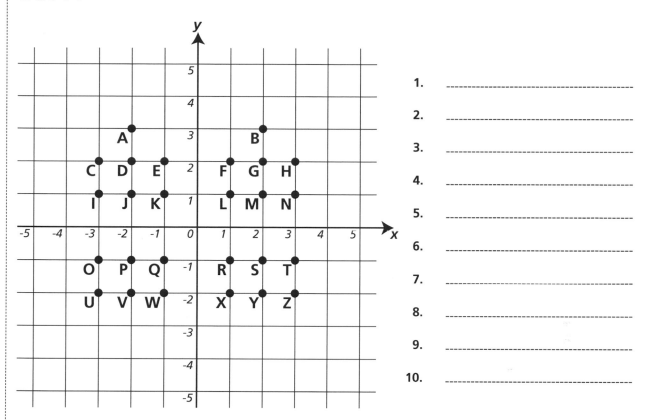

1. _____
2. _____
3. _____
4. _____
5. _____
6. _____
7. _____
8. _____
9. _____
10. _____

Mathematical Merry-go-round - Coordinate Words

Set B

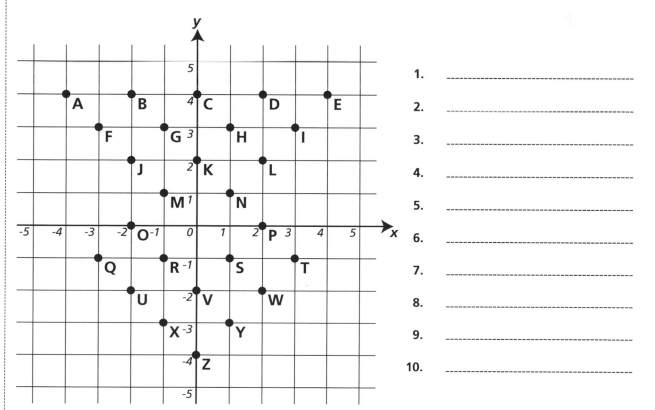

1. _____
2. _____
3. _____
4. _____
5. _____
6. _____
7. _____
8. _____
9. _____
10. _____

Mathematical Merry-go-round - Coordinate Words

Numberspell

This activity is an excellent way to practise the use of a number line and to encourage confidence in the handling of positive and negative numbers. The 'number snake' is in fact a number line with 26 positions and it is used initially to give a letter of the alphabet and then for counting onwards and backwards. Simple sums with positive and negative numbers lead a sequence of letters and thus a word, preferably a word from the mathematical vocabulary. Each page of photocopy masters opposite provides an alphabet snake for four pupils. It might be useful to make a permanent set by laminating the page before cutting it up into the individual units.

What does each pupil require?

A numberspell alphabet snake.
Pencil and paper or a whiteboard.

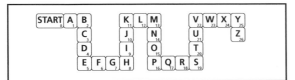

What does the teacher require?

Some suitable words with three, four or five letters and sums which lead to them.

Procedure:

Read out a sum which requires simple operations with positive and negative numbers. The first sum leads to the first letter of the word. Subsequent sums lead to an answer which has to be regarded as an operator, i.e. count forward or backwards that number of steps from the previous letter. It would be wise to use the word ARC below as an example.

It might be amusing to suggest the reverse process of converting a word into a single number. For example ARC is +1 +17 -15 = 3. How long before someone sees the short cut!

Three Letter Words

-7 + 8	-2 + 19	3 x -5
+1	+17	-15
A	**R**	**C**

-1 + 20	-9 + 11	-1 - 7
+19	+2	-8
S	**U**	**M**

-7 + 21	3 x -3	-2 + 17
+14	-9	+15
N	**E**	**T**

-4 + 6	7 - 8	-1 + 18
+2	-1	+17
B	**A**	**R**

-3 + 16	3 - 15	-1 + 16
+13	-12	+15
M	**A**	**P**

6 - (-6)	2 - 13	-3 + 25
+12	-11	+22
L	**A**	**W**

-6 + 20	9 - 14	1 - (-2)
+14	-5	+3
N	**I**	**L**

5 - (-10)	10 - 21	-1 + 1
+15	-11	+0
O	**D**	**D**

Four Letter Words

-6 + 7	-25 + 2	5 x -3	6 - (-4)
+1	+23	-15	+10
A	**X**	**I**	**S**

-3 + 8	1 x -1	-1 x -3	6 - 8
+5	-1	+3	-2
E	**D**	**G**	**E**

-5 + 13	2 - (-5)	2 - (-4)	-8 - (-5)
+8	+7	+6	-3
H	**O**	**U**	**R**

-1 + 14	-2 - 6	-6 - (-2)	-9 + 22
+13	-8	-4	+13
M	**E**	**A**	**N**

-3 x -4	-14 + 17	-4 - 8	5 - (-1)
+12	+3	-12	+6
L	**O**	**C**	**I**

-2 x -2	-4 + 9	2 x -3	-7 + 9
+4	+5	-6	+2
D	**I**	**C**	**E**

-2 x -13	7 x -3	-4 + 17	-1 - 2
+26	-21	+13	-3
Z	**E**	**R**	**O**

10 - (-9)	-2 x 4	-1 - 5	-9 x -2
+19	-8	-6	+18
S	**K**	**E**	**W**

Five Letter Words

-6 x -3	3 - 20	-1 + 20	-5 - 6	-2 x -3
+18	-17	+19	-11	+6
R	**A**	**T**	**I**	**O**

11 - (-5)	-6 - (-5)	-8 x -1	-9 - 9	-7 + 20
+16	-1	+8	-18	+13
P	**O**	**W**	**E**	**R**

-3 + 22	10 - 13	-7 - 4	-5 + 5	-12 + 11
+19	-3	-11	+0	-1
S	**P**	**E**	**E**	**D**

-3 x -3	-2 x -2	10 - 22	-1 x -6	-9 - (-7)
+9	+4	-12	+6	-2
I	**M**	**A**	**G**	**E**

-1 x -7	-4 + 15	4 - 21	-3 x -5	15 - 23
+7	+11	-17	+15	-8
G	**R**	**A**	**P**	**H**

-4 + 9	-3 + 20	-10 - 7	-3 x -3	-12 ÷ -2
+5	+17	-17	+9	+6
E	**V**	**E**	**N**	**T**

2 - (-3)	2 - (-10)	1 - (-3)	4 x -5	-12 + 23
+5	+12	+4	-20	+11
E	**Q**	**U**	**A**	**L**

8 - (-8)	-18 + 20	-10 + 1	-5 X -2	3 x -2
+16	+2	-9	+10	-6
P	**R**	**I**	**S**	**M**

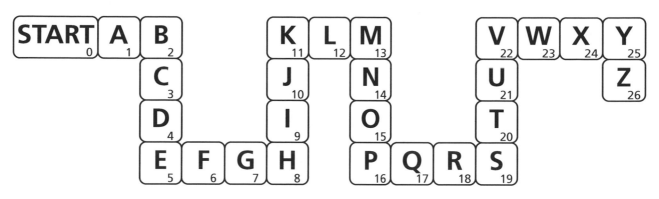

Mathematical Merry-go-round - Number spell

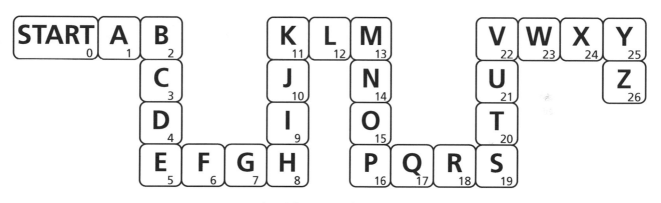

Mathematical Merry-go-round - Number spell

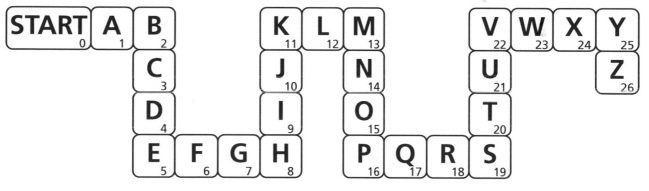

Mathematical Merry-go-round - Number spell

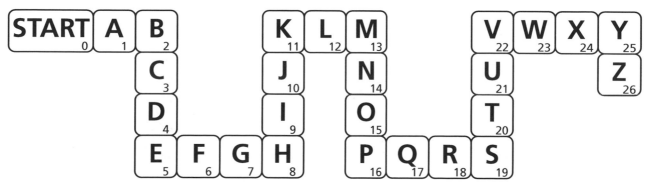

Mathematical Merry-go-round - Number spell

Fizz, Buzz

This is a very well known and ancient activity but no worse for that with the right class. Speed is of the essence and it is most important to keep the momentum going. A normal rule is that anyone who makes an error should drop out and let the others continue until no-one is left or you reach some target number.

What does each pupil require?
Alertness.

What does the teacher require?
Nothing really.
However the pair of charts here do enable you to keep track of where the counting has got to even in the face of laughter and loss of concentration.

Procedure:
Arrange the pupils around the outside of the room or in a horseshoe shape. For Fizz-Buzz they have to say 'Fizz' whenever the number is a multiple of three and 'Buzz' when it is a multiple of five. Multiples of fifteen become 'Fizz-Buzz'.

The second one is similar but uses the words 'Zip', 'Zap' for multiples of 3 and 5 and 'Pow' for multiples of 8. Multiples of 120 use all three words and 240 is a good number to end on. However, numbers up to 360 are given in case they are required.

1	1	41	41	FIZZ	81	121	121	161	161	FIZZ	201
2	2	FIZZ	42	82	82	122	122	FIZZ	162	202	202
FIZZ	3	43	43	83	83	FIZZ	123	163	163	203	203
4	4	44	44	FIZZ	84	124	124	164	164	FIZZ	204
BUZZ	5	FIZZ BUZZ	45	BUZZ	85	BUZZ	125	FIZZ BUZZ	165	BUZZ	205
FIZZ	6	46	46	86	86	FIZZ	126	166	166	206	206
7	7	47	47	FIZZ	87	127	127	167	167	FIZZ	207
8	8	FIZZ	48	88	88	128	128	FIZZ	168	208	208
FIZZ	9	49	49	89	89	FIZZ	129	169	169	209	209
BUZZ	10	BUZZ	50	FIZZ BUZZ	90	BUZZ	130	BUZZ	170	FIZZ BUZZ	210
11	11	FIZZ	51	91	91	131	131	FIZZ	171	211	211
FIZZ	12	52	52	92	92	FIZZ	132	172	172	212	212
13	13	53	53	FIZZ	93	133	133	173	173	FIZZ	213
14	14	FIZZ	54	94	94	134	134	FIZZ	174	214	214
FIZZ BUZZ	15	BUZZ	55	BUZZ	95	FIZZ BUZZ	135	BUZZ	175	BUZZ	215
16	16	56	56	FIZZ	96	136	136	176	176	FIZZ	216
17	17	FIZZ	57	97	97	137	137	FIZZ	177	217	217
FIZZ	18	58	58	98	98	FIZZ	138	178	178	218	218
19	19	59	59	FIZZ	99	139	139	179	179	FIZZ	219
BUZZ	20	FIZZ BUZZ	60	BUZZ	100	BUZZ	140	FIZZ BUZZ	180	BUZZ	210
FIZZ	21	61	61	101	101	FIZZ	141	181	181	221	221
22	22	62	62	FIZZ	102	142	142	182	182	FIZZ	222
23	23	FIZZ	63	103	103	143	143	FIZZ	183	223	223
FIZZ	24	64	64	104	104	FIZZ	144	184	184	224	224
BUZZ	25	BUZZ	65	FIZZ BUZZ	105	BUZZ	145	BUZZ	185	FIZZ BUZZ	225
26	26	FIZZ	66	106	106	146	146	FIZZ	186	226	226
FIZZ	27	67	67	107	107	FIZZ	147	187	187	227	227
28	28	68	68	FIZZ	108	148	148	188	188	FIZZ	228
29	29	FIZZ	69	109	109	149	149	FIZZ	189	229	229
FIZZ BUZZ	30	BUZZ	70	BUZZ	100	FIZZ BUZZ	150	BUZZ	190	BUZZ	230
31	31	71	71	FIZZ	111	151	151	191	191	FIZZ	231
32	32	FIZZ	72	112	112	152	152	FIZZ	192	232	232
FIZZ	33	73	73	113	113	FIZZ	153	193	193	233	233
34	34	74	74	FIZZ	114	154	154	194	194	FIZZ	234
BUZZ	35	FIZZ BUZZ	75	BUZZ	115	BUZZ	155	FIZZ BUZZ	195	BUZZ	235
FIZZ	36	76	76	116	116	FIZZ	156	196	196	236	236
37	37	77	77	FIZZ	117	157	157	197	197	FIZZ	237
38	38	FIZZ	78	118	118	158	158	FIZZ	198	238	238
FIZZ	39	79	79	119	119	FIZZ	159	199	199	239	239
BUZZ	40	BUZZ	80	FIZZ BUZZ	120	BUZZ	160	BUZZ	200	FIZZ BUZZ	240

Fizz Buzz

1	1	61	61	121	121	181	181	241	241	301	301
2	2	62	62	122	122	182	182	242	242	302	302
ZIP	3	ZIP	63	ZIP	123	ZIP	183	ZIP	243	ZIP	303
4	4	POW	64	124	124	POW	184	244	244	POW	304
ZAP	5	ZAP	65	ZAP	125	ZAP	185	ZAP	245	ZAP	305
ZIP	6	ZIP	66	ZIP	126	ZIP	186	ZIP	246	ZIP	306
7	7	67	67	127	127	187	187	247	247	307	307
POW	8	68	68	POW	128	188	188	POW	248	308	308
ZIP	9	ZIP	69	ZIP	129	ZIP	189	ZIP	249	ZIP	309
ZAP	10	ZAP	70	ZAP	130	ZAP	190	ZAP	250	ZAP	310
11	11	71	71	131	131	191	191	251	251	311	311
ZIP	12	ZIP POW	72	ZIP	132	ZIP POW	192	ZIP	252	ZIP POW	312
13	13	73	73	133	133	193	193	253	253	313	313
14	14	74	74	134	134	194	194	254	254	314	314
ZIP ZAP	15	ZIP ZAP	75	ZIP ZAP	135	ZIP ZAP	195	ZIP ZAP	255	ZIP ZAP	315
POW	16	76	76	POW	136	196	196	POW	256	316	316
17	17	77	77	137	137	197	197	257	257	317	317
ZIP	18	ZIP	78	ZIP	138	ZIP	198	ZIP	258	ZIP	318
19	19	79	79	139	139	199	199	259	259	319	319
ZAP	20	ZAP POW	80	ZAP	140	ZAP POW	200	ZAP	260	ZAP POW	320
ZIP	21	ZIP	81	ZIP	141	ZIP	201	ZIP	261	ZIP	321
22	22	82	82	142	142	202	202	262	262	322	322
23	23	83	83	143	143	203	203	263	263	323	323
ZIP POW	24	ZIP	84	ZIP POW	144	ZIP	204	ZIP POW	264	ZIP	324
ZAP	25	ZAP	85	ZAP	145	ZAP	205	ZAP	265	ZAP	325
26	26	86	86	146	146	206	206	266	266	326	326
ZIP	27	ZIP	87	ZIP	147	ZIP	207	ZIP	267	ZIP	327
28	28	POW	88	148	148	POW	208	268	268	POW	328
29	29	89	89	149	149	209	209	269	269	329	329
ZIP ZAP	30	ZIP ZAP	90	ZIP ZAP	150	ZIP ZAP	210	ZIP ZAP	270	ZIP ZAP	330
31	31	91	91	151	151	211	211	271	271	331	331
POW	32	92	92	POW	152	212	212	POW	272	332	332
ZIP	33	ZIP	93	ZIP	153	ZIP	213	ZIP	273	ZIP	333
34	34	94	94	154	154	214	214	274	274	334	334
ZAP	35	ZAP	95	ZAP	155	ZAP	215	ZAP	275	ZAP	335
ZIP	36	ZIP POW	96	ZIP	156	ZIP POW	216	ZIP	276	ZIP POW	336
37	37	97	97	157	157	217	217	277	277	337	337
38	38	98	98	158	158	218	218	278	278	338	338
ZIP	39	ZIP	99	ZIP	159	ZIP	219	ZIP	279	ZIP	339
ZAP POW	40	ZAP	100	ZAP POW	160	ZAP	210	ZAP POW	280	ZAP	340
41	41	101	101	161	161	221	221	281	281	341	341
ZIP	42	ZIP	102	ZIP	162	ZIP	222	ZIP	282	ZIP	342
43	43	103	103	163	163	223	223	283	283	343	343
44	44	POW	104	164	164	POW	224	284	284	POW	344
ZIP ZAP	45	ZIP ZAP	105	ZIP ZAP	165	ZIP ZAP	225	ZIP ZAP	285	ZIP ZAP	345
46	46	106	106	166	166	226	226	286	286	346	346
47	47	107	107	167	167	227	227	287	287	347	347
ZIP POW	48	ZIP	108	ZIP POW	168	ZIP	228	ZIP POW	288	ZIP	348
49	49	109	109	169	169	229	229	289	289	349	349
ZAP	50	ZAP	100	ZAP	170	ZAP	230	ZAP	290	ZAP	350
ZIP	51	ZIP	111	ZIP	171	ZIP	231	ZIP	291	ZIP	351
52	52	POW	112	172	172	POW	232	292	292	POW	352
53	53	113	113	173	173	233	233	293	293	353	353
ZIP	54	ZIP	114	ZIP	174	ZIP	234	ZIP	294	ZIP	354
ZAP	55	ZAP	115	ZAP	175	ZAP	235	ZAP	295	ZAP	355
POW	56	116	116	POW	176	236	236	POW	296	356	356
ZIP	57	ZIP	117	ZIP	177	ZIP	237	ZIP	297	ZIP	357
58	58	118	118	178	178	238	238	298	298	358	358
59	59	119	119	179	179	239	239	299	299	359	359
ZIP ZAP	60	ZIP ZAP POW	120	ZIP ZAP	180	ZIP ZAP POW	240	ZIP ZAP	300	ZIP ZAP POW	360

The Drawing Game

This is an excellent activity for testing and reinforcing mathematical vocabulary and it is an easy one to check and for the pupils to compare their diagrams with those of their neighbours. Six examples are given here but it is not difficult to construct further ones to meet the needs of particular classes.

Since constructing such sets of instructions does demand clarity and precision of thought it works well in reverse. Ask the pupils to construct a drawing of their own together with a set of unambiguous instructions. They can then test out their sets of instructions on others.

What does each pupil require?
Possibly a set of drawing instruments and some blank paper.
Alternatively, a small whiteboard and pen.

What does the teacher require?
Sets of instructions which lead to interesting diagrams.

Procedure:
Read out the sets of instructions in a measured way and at an appropriate speed. Probably it is best to compare the resulting diagrams after each one has been completed.

Since it is geometrical vocabulary which is really being worked upon and not the accuracy of measurement, it might be preferable only to allow freehand drawing, even of circles.

The measurements are given simply to produce diagrams of a reasonably convenient size. It might be best to point out the meaning of 'horizontal' and 'vertical' in the sets of instructions.

Although topics for possible discussion are given, it is probably best to limit such comments to passing remarks.

Diagram 1

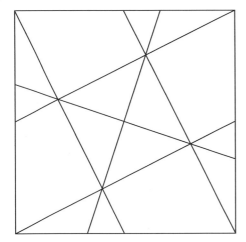

The instructions
All the lines are straight.
1. Draw a square of side roughly 8cm.
2. Join the mid-point of the base to the top left corner.
3. Join the mid-point of the left side to the top right corner.
4. Join the mid-point of the top to the bottom right corner.
5. Join the mid-point of the right side to the bottom left corner.
6. Draw in the two diagonals of the new central square and continue the lines until they reach the edges of the original square.

Possible discussion: Rotational Symmetry

Diagram 2

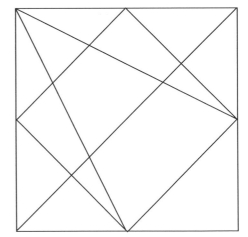

The instructions
All the lines are straight.
1. Draw a square of side roughly 10cm
2. Join the mid-point of the base to the top left corner.
3. Join the mid-point of the right side of the square to the top left hand corner.
4. Draw the diagonal from the top right hand corner to the bottom left hand corner.
5. Join the mid-points of the adjacent sides of the square - four lines.

Possible discussion: Reflectional Symmetry

The Drawing Game

Diagram 3

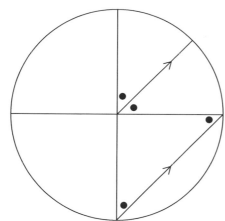

The instructions

1. Draw a circle of radius about 5 cm.

From now on all the lines are straight

2. Draw a diameter parallel to the bottom edge of the paper.
3. Draw a second diameter at right angles to the first.
4. Draw a chord joining the bottom of the vertical diameter to the right hand end of the horizontal diameter.
5. Draw a radius parallel to this in the top right hand sector of the circle.
6. Mark all 45° angles with a dot.
7. Mark parallel lines with arrows.

Possible discussion:
Alternate and corresponding angles

Diagram 5

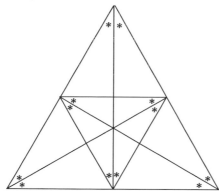

The instructions

All the lines are straight

1. Draw a equilateral triangle of side roughly 9cm.
2. Join the mid-points of each pair of adjacent sides - 3 lines.
3. Join the mid-point of each side to its opposite angle - 3 sides.
4. Mark all 30° angles with a star.

Possible discussion:
Equilateral, right angled and isosceles triangles

Diagram 4

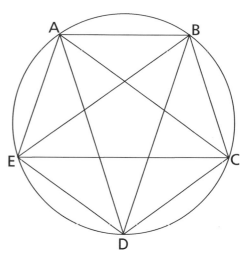

The instructions

1. Draw a circle of radius about 5cm.

From now on all the lines are straight.

2. Mark five points on the circumference which are equidistant from each other and label them A B C D E.
3. Join every point to every other point - ten lines.

Possible discussion: The names of polygon shapes:

ABCDE	Pentagon
ABCE	Trapezium
ABD	Isosceles Triangle

Diagram 6

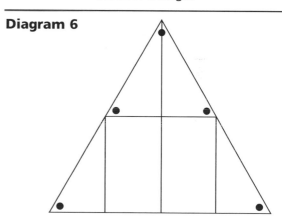

The instructions

All the lines are straight

1. Draw a equilateral triangle of side roughly 8cm, with the base horizontal.
2. Join the top to the mid-point of the base.
3. Half way up this line draw a line across the triangle horizontally.
4. Where this line meets the sides of the triangle draw two vertical lines down to the base.
5. Mark all 60° angles with a dot.

Possible discussion: Similar triangles

Bearing Words

This activity is a very good one for practising either estimating or measuring bearings from one point to another. Probably it is more useful in a classroom situation to place the emphasis on estimating and the linking lines of the diagram are sufficiently well separated to make this possible. If you have an overhead projector, then everyone can work from the same image and the grid of parallel north lines will help the participants to make sensible estimates. If you prefer to work with photocopies, then it would also be possible to use this activity for angle measurer practice. The diagram is accurate and all angles are whole numbers of degrees.

What does each pupil require?
A photocopy of the diagram opposite, showing points connected by lines on a grid of north lines.

If you would prefer the pupils to measure the bearings exactly then each pupil needs a protractor or a 360° angle measurer.

They could also answer on whiteboards.

What does the teacher require?
A set of questions and their answers.
Possibly an overhead projector.

Procedure:
Read out the first letter and then the two, three or four bearings to complete the spelling of the word.

Pupils should be reminded that bearings are always measured clockwise from north and given as three figures.

You might wish to include this modest little joke. 'I am seven degrees clockwise from north. Who am I?' Answer: James Bond (007)

Set A		
Questions		Answers
1. B 154° 309°		BED
2. B 111° 202°		BAG
3. A 058° 201°		ACE
4. A 202° 047°		AGE
5. C 238° 190° 020°		CAKE
6. B 154° 000° 239°		BEAD
7. M 339° 239° 129°		MADE
8. F 286° 058° 201°		FACE
9. C 238° 202° 047°		CAGE
10. H 296° 000° 239°		HEAD

Set B		
Questions		Answers
1. C 238° 291°		CAB
2. F 286° 239°		FAD
3. B 154° 227°		BEG
4. D 059° 239°		DAD
5. K 020° 227°		KEG
6. F 286° 190° 020°		FAKE
7. A 058° 170° 296°		ACHE
8. E 309° 175° 047°		EDGE
9. B 154° 000° 058° 170°		BEACH
10. B 111° 239° 175° 047°		BADGE

Making up more Bearing Words
The chart below shows in alphabetical order, the bearings of letter combinations which are most likely to lead to useful short words and will help in the preparation of further sets of words.

A to B	A to C	A to D	A to E	A to F	A to G	A to K	A to M	B to A	B to E	C to A	C to E
291°	058°	239°	180°	106°	202°	190°	159°	111°	154°	238°	201°

C to H	D to A	D to E	D to G	E to A	E to B	E to C	E to D	E to F	E to G	E to H	E to K
170°	059°	129°	175°	000°	334°	021°	309°	051°	227°	116°	200°

E to M	F to A	F to E	G to A	G to D	G to E	H to C	H to E	K to A	K to E	M to A	M to E
138°	286°	231°	022°	355°	047°	350°	296°	010°	020°	339°	318°

Notice how reverse bearings are related. For example the bearings of (B to A) and (A to B) differ by 180°.

Bearings are always measured clockwise from North

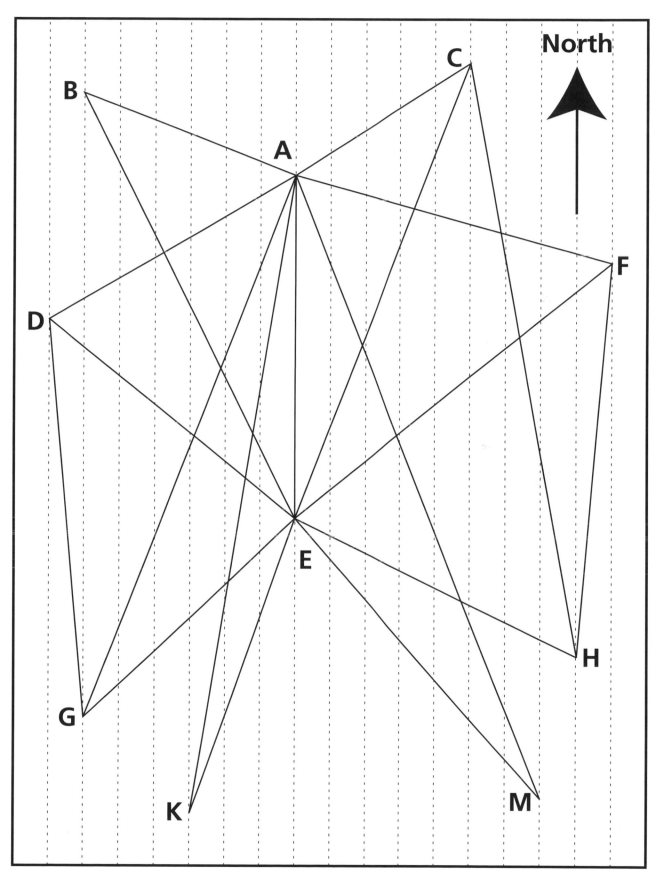

Mathematical Bingo

The key step in this mathematical version of Bingo is that the pupils make their own Bingo cards. It is a good activity for reinforcing topics where there are several ways of expressing the same number in different forms, for instance fractions, decimals and percentages. On page 24 there are 12 photocopiable pupil cards and on page 23 a blank set of master grids so that you can easily construct additional sets of questions and answers.

What does each pupil require?

A blank 4 x 3 Bingo card to fill in, possibly counters to cover correct answers. Alternatively a coloured pen or pencil to mark them off. Several games could be played with the same card and the same set of questions using different colours.

Pupils could also play on more than one card at one time.

What does the teacher require?

A pupils' master card.
A teacher's question set.
An overhead projector or blackboard.
If you make two copies of the teacher's question set and cut one up into the individual units, they can be placed in a container to be chosen at random. Then each question used can be placed in position on the other copy and used to check a winning claim.

Procedure:

Issue a blank 4 x 3 Bingo card to each pupil. Then project on to a screen or copy on to a blackboard a complete 8 x 3 answer set. Everyone then has to choose for themselves just four possible answers from each row and to write them in to the appropriate squares of their own blank card. Everyone has then created their own card with twelve of the twenty-four numbers on it. It is likely but not absolutely certain that all will be different.

To play the game, call out one of the three alternative questions in a square and ask the pupils to mark the correct answer if they have it. Continue until someone has a completed card.

Teacher Question Set A: Mental Arithmetic

12	18	20	24	28	30	32	35
3 x 4	2 x 9	4 x 5	8 x 3	4 x 7	6 x 5	8 x 4	7 x 5
Half of 24	3^2 x 2	100 ÷ 5	6 x 4	2 x 14	3 x 10	16 x 2	Half of 70
$\sqrt{144}$	36 ÷ 2	$\sqrt{400}$	2 x 12	Half of 56	Quarter of 120	2^5	100 - 65
36	**40**	**42**	**45**	**48**	**50**	**54**	**60**
9 x 4	8 x 5	6 x 7	9 x 5	6 x 8	5 x 10	6 x 9	6 x 10
6^2	4 x 10	3 x 14	3 x 15	4 x 12	2 x 25	3 x 18	5 x 12
$10^2 - 8^2$	$6^2 + 2^2$	2 x 21	Half of 90	3 x 16	$7^2 + 1^2$	2 x 27	$8^2 - 2^2$
66	**72**	**80**	**81**	**84**	**90**	**96**	**100**
6 x 11	9 x 8	8 x 10	9 x 9	12 x 7	10 x 9	12 x 8	10 x 10
3 x 22	12 x 6	4 x 20	3 x 27	6 x 14	6 x 15	6 x 16	5 x 20
100 - 34	3 x 24	5 x 16	3^4	3 x 28	2 x 45	$10^2 - 2^2$	$6^2 + 8^2$

Mathematical Bingo

Answer Set A: Mental Arithmetic

12	18	20	24	28	30	32	35
36	40	42	45	48	50	54	60
66	72	80	81	84	90	96	100

Answer Set B: Decimals

0.1	0.2	0.3	0.4	0.5	0.6	0.7	0.8
0.01	0.02	0.03	0.04	0.05	0.06	0.07	0.08
0.9	0.09	0.25	0.75	0.99	0.15	0.35	0.95

Answer Set C: Negative Numbers

-12	-11	-10	-9	-8	-7	-6	-5
-4	-3	-2	-1	0	+1	+2	+3
+4	+5	+6	+8	+12	+15	+20	+24

Answer Set D: Powers and Roots

1	2	3	4	5	6	7	8
10	12	13	15	64	81	100	121
144	169	196	225	256	324	400	900

Mathematical Bingo

Teacher Question Set B: Decimals

0.1	**0.2**	**0.3**	**0.4**	**0.5**	**0.6**	**0.7**	**0.8**
$\frac{1}{10}$	$\frac{1}{5}$	$\frac{3}{10}$	$\frac{2}{5}$	$\frac{1}{2}$	$\frac{3}{5}$	$\frac{7}{10}$	$\frac{4}{5}$
10%	20%	30%	40%	50%	60%	70%	80%
0.4 ÷ 4	2 ÷ 10	6 ÷ 20	40 ÷ 100	2 x 0.25	0.06 x 10	0.35 x 2	16 ÷ 20
0.01	**0.02**	**0.03**	**0.04**	**0.05**	**0.06**	**0.07**	**0.08**
$\frac{1}{100}$	$\frac{1}{50}$	$\frac{3}{100}$	$\frac{1}{25}$	$\frac{1}{20}$	$\frac{3}{50}$	$\frac{7}{100}$	$\frac{2}{25}$
1%	2%	3%	4%	5%	6%	7%	8%
0.1^2	20 ÷ 1000	0.1 x 0.3	0.2 x 0.2	0.5 ÷ 10	0.3 x 0.2	0.7 x 0.1	0.2 x 0.4
0.9	**0.09**	**0.25**	**0.75**	**0.99**	**0.15**	**0.35**	**0.95**
$\frac{9}{10}$	$\frac{9}{100}$	$\frac{1}{4}$	$\frac{3}{4}$	$\frac{99}{100}$	$\frac{3}{20}$	$\frac{7}{20}$	$\frac{19}{20}$
90%	9%	25%	75%	99%	15%	35%	95%
0.45 x 2	0.3^2	Half^2	0.25 x 3	1 - 0.01	0.3 x 0.5	0.5 x 0.7	1 - 0.05

Teacher Question Set C: Negative Numbers

-12	**-11**	**-10**	**-9**	**-8**	**-7**	**-6**	**-5**
-4 - 8	-5 - 6	-2 - 8	6 - 15	-10 + 2	-3 - 4	4 - 10	-1 - 4
2 x -6	3 - 14	-5 x 2	3 x -3	4 x -2	-9 + 2	-2 x 3	-7 - (-2)
20 - 32	-8 - 3	-12 + 2	-14 + 5	3 - 11	-10 - (-3)	-18 ÷ 3	7 - 12
-4	**-3**	**-2**	**-1**	**0**	**+1**	**+2**	**+3**
6 - 10	3 - 6	-5 + 3	11 - 12	-6 + 6	-7 + 8	-3 + 5	-8 + 11
-8 - (-4)	12 ÷ -4	-10 ÷ 5	$(-1)^3$	-1 - (-1)	$(-1)^4$	-8 ÷ -4	1 - (-2)
-2 x 2	-5 - (-2)	7 - 9	-8 + 7	3 + (-3)	-4 ÷ (-4)	-7 + 9	-12 ÷ (-4)
+4	**+5**	**+6**	**+8**	**+12**	**+15**	**+20**	**+24**
-2 + 6	-5 + 10	-10 + 16	-2 x -4	-2 x -6	-3 x -5	-2 x -10	-8 x -3
$(-2)^2$	-50 ÷ -10	2 - (-4)	-16 ÷ -2	4 - (-8)	8 - (-7)	-3 + 23	-6 x -4
-9 + 13	-1 x -5	-18 ÷ (-3)	-6 + 14	-1 + 13	-30 ÷ (-2)	-4 x -5	-6 + 30

Mathematical Bingo

Teacher Question Set D: Powers and Roots

1	**2**	**3**	**4**	**5**	**6**	**7**	**8**
1^{10}	$\sqrt{4}$	$\sqrt{9}$	$\sqrt{16}$	$\sqrt{25}$	$\sqrt{36}$	$4^2 - 3^2$	$\sqrt{64}$
4^0	$\sqrt[3]{8}$	$\sqrt[3]{27}$	$\sqrt[3]{64}$	$\sqrt[3]{125}$	$\sqrt[3]{216}$	$\sqrt{49}$	$(\sqrt{4})^3$
$2 - 1^{13}$	$\sqrt[5]{32}$	$\sqrt{100} - \sqrt{49}$	$2^3 - 2^2$	$3^2 - 2^2$	$\sqrt{4} \times \sqrt{9}$	$\sqrt{121} - \sqrt{16}$	$(2\sqrt{2})^2$
10	**12**	**13**	**15**	**64**	**81**	**100**	**121**
$\sqrt{100}$	$\sqrt{144}$	$\sqrt{169}$	$\sqrt{225}$	8^2	9^2	10^2	11^2
$\sqrt[3]{1000}$	$\sqrt{9} \times 2^2$	$2^2 + 3^2$	$\sqrt{25} \times \sqrt{9}$	4^3	3^4	$\sqrt{10000}$	$10^2 + 5^2 - 2^2$
$\sqrt{900} - \sqrt{400}$	$2^3 + 2^2$	$4^2 - \sqrt{9}$	$\sqrt{400} - \sqrt{25}$	$10^2 - 6^2$	$15^2 - 12^2$	$6^2 + 8^2$	$5^3 - 2^2$
144	**169**	**196**	**225**	**256**	**324**	**400**	**900**
12^2	13^2	14^2	15^2	16^2	18^2	20^2	30^2
$6^2 \times \sqrt{16}$	$12^2 + 5^2$	$7^2 \times 2^2$	$12^2 + 9^2$	4^4	$9^2 \times \sqrt{16}$	$16^2 + 12^2$	$10^3 - 10^2$
$3^2 \times 4^2$	$10 \times 4^2 + 3^2$	$6^3 - \sqrt{400}$	$3^2 \times 5^2$	2^8	$\sqrt{81} \times 6^2$	$2^4 \times 5^2$	$5^2 \times 6^2$

Blank Masters

Mathematical Bingo

Mathematical Merry-go-round - Mathematical Bingo

Mathematical Merry-go-round - Mathematical Bingo

Mathematical Merry-go-round - Mathematical Bingo

Mathematical Merry-go-round - Mathematical Bingo

Mathematical Merry-go-round - Mathematical Bingo

Mathematical Merry-go-round - Mathematical Bingo

Mathematical Merry-go-round - Mathematical Bingo

Mathematical Merry-go-round - Mathematical Bingo

Mathematical Merry-go-round - Mathematical Bingo

Mathematical Merry-go-round - Mathematical Bingo

Mathematical Merry-go-round - Mathematical Bingo

Mathematical Merry-go-round - Mathematical Bingo

Multiplication First

Like many good games of chance, this game has a very nice 'strategic' feel to it. A good sensible strategy will undoubtedly help, but the final results will still be strongly affected by the way the numbers actually fall. It is most important that everyone enters each number as soon as it is called out.

Each set requires 18 numbers and their production can be speeded up by throwing a pair of dice and by calling out the number on the die closest to you first. Alternatively, you can use the sets of 'fixed' random numbers listed below. It is easy to create such lists by throwing some dice before the lesson begins.

What does each pupil require?
A blank master sheet obtained by enlarging the lower half of this page by 141%.

What does the teacher require?
Either a pair of 1 to 6 dice, or a pair of 0 to 9 dice and a simple shaker.

Alternatively, use a list of 18 'random' numbers prepared in advance. Below are two possible groups of 18 numbers for each set.

Using 1 to 6 normal dice
Set 1   1, 6, 2, 4, 4, 3, 4, 5, 6, 3, 5, 5, 2, 1, 6, 1, 2, 6
Set 2   3, 4, 4, 6, 5, 3, 3, 5, 3, 1, 4, 2, 4, 5, 2, 6, 1, 2

Using 0 to 9 decimal 10-sided dice
Set 1   6, 3, 9, 3, 4, 0, 0, 6, 1, 1, 1, 5, 3, 4, 9, 9, 8, 7
Set 2   2, 8, 2, 4, 6, 3, 3, 0, 9, 6, 4, 7, 4, 2, 5, 8, 7, 6

Procedure:
Call out the group of 18 numbers one at a time and ask the pupils to enter each into one of the 18 spaces in the five grids. The aim is to obtain the highest possible total score.

When the list is complete, do each of the five sums and add them to get the grand total. Remind them that multiplications are always completed before the additions and subtractions.

If this game proves popular, try the variation of asking them to place the numbers so as to obtain the lowest possible grand total.

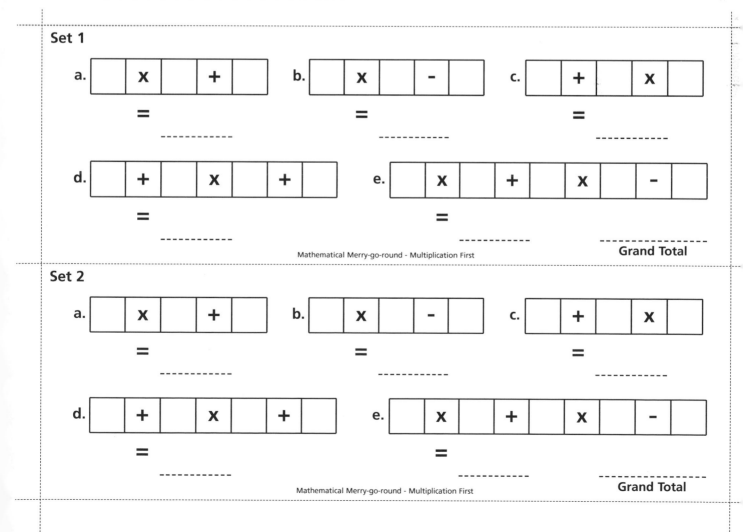

True or False

This activity is a simple and quick way to revise simple arithmetic or simple algebra. The statements which are either true or false need to be fairly short as everything has to be held in the memory. Two trial activities with 24 and 30 statements are given below and they can be used to test the format. If you use red paper for 'false' and green paper for 'true', it rather suggests the 'stop' and 'go' of traffic lights.

What does each pupil require?
Two cards, one showing the word 'true' and the other showing the word 'false'.

What does the teacher require?
A suitable set of questions and their answers.

Procedure:
Read out one question at a time and ask for an instant display of the correct card.

When the answer is false, ask one pupil to say why.

It does not take long to construct a set of true or false statements on virtually any mathematical topic.

Set A: Metric Units

1. $30\,mm = 0.3\,m$	F (0.03)	13. $1250\,g = 1.25\,kg$	T
2. $6\,cm = 60\,mm$	T	14. $60\,g = 6000\,mg$	F (60,000)
3. $0.5\,m = 50\,mm$	F (500)	15. $50\,ml = 0.5$ litres	F (0.05)
4. $40\,cm = 0.4\,m$	T	16. $200\,cl = 0.2$ litres	F (2)
5. $30\,m = 0.3\,km$	F (0.03)	17. $150\,ml = 0.15$ litres	T
6. $8\,m = 0.0008\,km$	F (0.008)	18. $10\,000\,m^2 = 1$ hectare	T
7. $100\,mm^2 = 1\,cm^2$	T	19. $20\,000\,ml = 2$ litres	F (20)
8. $100\,cm^2 = 1\,m^2$	F (0.01)	20. $75\,ml = 7.5\,cl$	T
9. $1\,000\,000\,cm^3 = 1\,m^3$	T	21. $1000\,m^2 = 1\,km^2$	F (0.001)
10. $40\,mg = 0.04\,g$	T	22. $1000\,W = 1\,kW$	T
11. $10\,000\,mg = 1\,kg$	F (0.01)	23. 10 million $mm = 1\,km$	F (10)
12. $50\,kg = 0.5$ Tonnes	F (0.05)	24. 1 billion $mg = 1$ Tonne	T

Set B: Indices

1. $4^2 = 16$	T	16. $5^2 + 5^2 = 1^2 + 7^2$	T
2. $3^2 = 6$	F (9 ≠ 6)	17. $8^2 - 6^2 = 4^2$	F (28 ≠ 16)
3. $2^2 \times 4^2 = 8^4$	F (64 ≠ 4096)	18. $2^3 = 6$	F (8 ≠ 6)
4. $a^2 \times a^3 = a^5$	T	19. $2^4 = 16$	T
5. $a \times a^2 = a^3$	T	20. $\sqrt{(4^3)} = 2^5$	F (8 ≠ 32)
6. $1^2 + 2^2 = 3^2$	F (5 ≠ 9)	21. $2a^2 \times 3a^2 = 6a^4$	T
7. $1^3 + 2^3 = 3^2$	T	22. $4b^2 \times 2b^3 = 8b^5$	T
8. $2^3 \times 2^5 = 4^8$	F (256 ≠ 65536)	23. $12a^6 \div 6a^2 = 2a^4$	T
9. $5^2 \times 5^3 = 5^5$	T	24. $3a^3 \times 2a^2 = 6a^6$	F ($6a^5 \neq 6a^6$)
10. $3^5 \div 3^3 = 3^2$	T	25. $8a^8 \div 2a^2 = 4a^4$	F ($4a^6 \neq 4a^4$)
11. $2^7 \div 2^6 = 1^1$	F (2 ≠ 1)	26. $a \times b \times c = c \times b \times a$	T
12. $6^2 \div 3^2 = 3^1$	F (4 ≠ 3)	27. $a \times b \div c = c \times b \div a$	F (ab/c ≠ cb/a)
13. $3^2 + 4^2 = 5^2$	T	28. $2a \times 3b \times 3c = 12abc$	T
14. $4^2 + 5^2 = 6^2$	F (41 ≠ 36)	29. $2a \times 3b \times 4a = 24a^2b$	T
15. $10^2 - 8^2 = 6^2$	T	30. $\sqrt{(100^3)} = \sqrt[3]{(100^2)}$	F ($1000 \neq \sqrt[3]{10000}$)

True

Mathematical Merry-go-round - True or False

True

Mathematical Merry-go-round - True or False

True

Mathematical Merry-go-round - True or False

True

Mathematical Merry-go-round - True or False

False

Mathematical Merry-go-round - True or False

False

Mathematical Merry-go-round - True or False

False

Mathematical Merry-go-round - True or False

False

Mathematical Merry-go-round - True or False

Memory Game

This activity works best if the pupils sit in a circular or horse-shoe arrangement around the room. It offers a fun way of revising and repeating simple formulae and simple relationships. For the set of cards below there should be an even number of pupils in the circle because the format is rather like a question and answer on alternate cards. If you have an odd number, then pupil 1 should be given the first two cards. He or she has only a small part to play and the fact that it is doubled is not significant. The supplied cards are for 20 pupils and this offers a lot for pupil 20 to remember but it can be done! Usually it is best to split larger groups into smaller ones of say a dozen of fourteen or so. Generally it best to remove earlier cards from the set rather than the later ones, but that will rather depend on the ability of the class.

What does each pupil require?

The correctly numbered card. Obtain them by enlarging each of the sets of masters by 141%. A more robust class set can be made by laminating the sheet before cutting up the individual cards.

What does the teacher require?

Strictly nothing except a good memory.
However, it will be helpful to have the lists showing what is on all the cards and their order in clear sight.

Procedure:

A set of cards is handed out in order around the class. The first person reads out what is on card 1. Pupil 2 says what pupil 1 has said and then adds what is on card 2. Pupil 3 repeats what pupils 1 & 2 have both said and adds the contents of card 3. Pupil 4 says what the previous three have said in the right order and adds the new contribution. So it continues until everyone has had their turn

Gradually it gets harder and harder but because they are facing each other in a circular arrangement there is plenty to help jog the memory. However, rather than let the whole thing descend into silence and embarrassment at any point, let the pupil who's contribution has been forgotten act as a prompt.

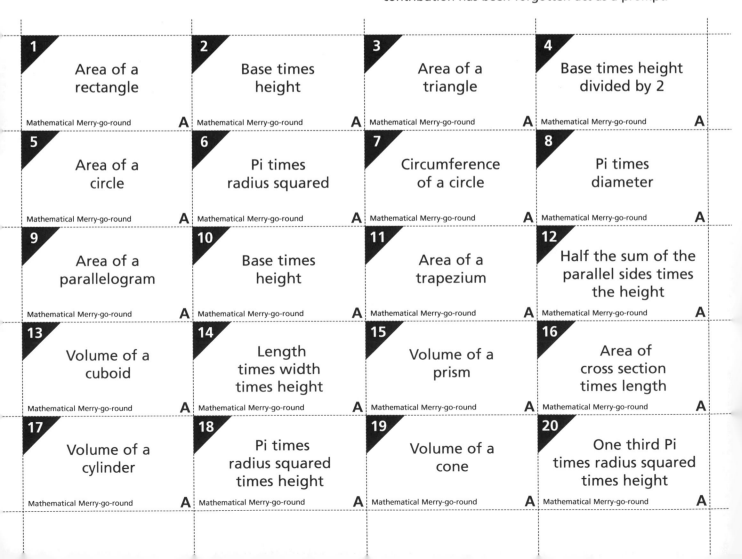

1 Area of a rectangle	2 Base times height	3 Area of a triangle	4 Base times height divided by 2
Mathematical Merry-go-round	Mathematical Merry-go-round	Mathematical Merry-go-round	Mathematical Merry-go-round
5 Area of a circle	6 Pi times radius squared	7 Circumference of a circle	8 Pi times diameter
Mathematical Merry-go-round	Mathematical Merry-go-round	Mathematical Merry-go-round	Mathematical Merry-go-round
9 Area of a parallelogram	10 Base times height	11 Area of a trapezium	12 Half the sum of the parallel sides times the height
Mathematical Merry-go-round	Mathematical Merry-go-round	Mathematical Merry-go-round	Mathematical Merry-go-round
13 Volume of a cuboid	14 Length times width times height	15 Volume of a prism	16 Area of cross section times length
Mathematical Merry-go-round	Mathematical Merry-go-round	Mathematical Merry-go-round	Mathematical Merry-go-round
17 Volume of a cylinder	18 Pi times radius squared times height	19 Volume of a cone	20 One third Pi times radius squared times height
Mathematical Merry-go-round	Mathematical Merry-go-round	Mathematical Merry-go-round	Mathematical Merry-go-round

Memory Game

1 $1^2 = 1$	**2** $2^2 = 4$	**3** $3^2 = 9$	**4** $4^2 = 16$
B Mathematical Merry-go-round	B Mathematical Merry-go-round	B Mathematical Merry-go-round	B Mathematical Merry-go-round
5 $5^2 = 25$	**6** $6^2 = 36$	**7** $7^2 = 49$	**8** $8^2 = 64$
B Mathematical Merry-go-round	B Mathematical Merry-go-round	B Mathematical Merry-go-round	B Mathematical Merry-go-round
9 $9^2 = 81$	**10** $10^2 = 100$	**11** $11^2 = 121$	**12** $12^2 = 144$
B Mathematical Merry-go-round	B Mathematical Merry-go-round	B Mathematical Merry-go-round	B Mathematical Merry-go-round
13 $13^2 = 169$	**14** $14^2 = 196$	**15** $15^2 = 225$	**16** $16^2 = 256$
B Mathematical Merry-go-round	B Mathematical Merry-go-round	B Mathematical Merry-go-round	B Mathematical Merry-go-round
17 $17^2 = 289$	**18** $18^2 = 324$	**19** $19^2 = 361$	**20** $20^2 = 400$
B Mathematical Merry-go-round	B Mathematical Merry-go-round	B Mathematical Merry-go-round	B Mathematical Merry-go-round

Set A

Card 1: Area of a rectangle
Card 2: Base times height
Card 3: Area of a triangle
Card 4: Base times height divided by 2
Card 5: Area of a circle
Card 6: Pi times radius squared
Card 7: Circumference of a circle
Card 8: Pi times diameter
Card 9: Area of a parallelogram
Card 10: Base times height
Card 11: Area of a trapezium
Card 12: Half the sum of the parallel sides times the height
Card 13: Volume of a cuboid
Card 14: Length times width times height
Card 15: Volume of a prism
Card 16: Area of cross section times length
Card 17: Volume of a cylinder
Card 18: Pi times radius squared times height
Card 19: Volume of a cone
Card 20: One third Pi times radius squared times height

Set B

Card 1: $1^2 = 1$
Card 2: $2^2 = 4$
Card 3: $3^2 = 9$
Card 4: $4^2 = 16$
Card 5: $5^2 = 25$
Card 6: $6^2 = 36$
Card 7: $7^2 = 49$
Card 8: $8^2 = 64$
Card 9: $9^2 = 81$
Card 10: $10^2 = 100$
Card 11: $11^2 = 121$
Card 12: $12^2 = 144$
Card 13: $13^2 = 169$
Card 14: $14^2 = 196$
Card 15: $15^2 = 225$
Card 16: $16^2 = 256$
Card 17: $17^2 = 289$
Card 18: $18^2 = 324$
Card 19: $19^2 = 361$
Card 20: $20^2 = 400$

Data Handling

Extracting information from tables and charts is a very useful skill and this activity offers some varied practice at doing so. The information sheet opposite gives eight pieces of data about a group of 25 girls from years 11 and 12 of a certain school. It is rather convenient that there is no-one whose name begins with Q and so it becomes a simple matter to calculate the percentages of the complete group who have or share particular characteristics without the need for a calculator.

What does each pupil require?
A data handling information sheet.
Some paper or a whiteboard to note down the answers.

What does the teacher require?
A data handling information sheet.
A list of suitable questions and their answers relating to the sheet.

Procedure:
Read out questions one at a time and get the pupils to write down their answers individually. It is probably best to halt after each group of five and compare answers.

If you want to take things further you can discuss with the class whether certain characteristics might go together, for instance, do tall people have big feet and so on.

The data could also be used for graph plotting and work on mean, median and mode.

Questions	Answers	
1. Who is the oldest girl in year 11?	Jenny	
2. Who is the youngest girl in year 12?	Tanya	
3. How many 'only children' are there?	8	
4. What percentage are 'only children'?	32%	
5. How many left handed children are there?	6	
6. What percentage are right handed?	76%	
7. What fraction of the girls are in year 11?	3/5	
8. What percentage them are in year 12?	40%	
9. Who is the shortest person in year 11?	Gemma	
10. Who is the tallest person in year 12?	Ursula	
11. Who has the greatest arm span in year 11?	Irene	
12. Who has the smallest arm span in year 12?	Sally	
13. Who has the smallest feet in year 11?	Gemma	
14. Who has the biggest feet in year 12?	Ursula	
15. Who comes from the biggest family?	Sally	
16. Could Gemma and Hayley be twins?	No	
17. Who is taller than Ursula?	Anna	
18. Who is the youngest pupil of all?	Carol	
19. Who is the oldest pupil of all?	Yvonne	
20. How many of year 11 are right handed?	11	
21. How many of year 12 are right handed?	8	
22. Which year has a greater proportion of right handed pupils?	Year 12	(8/10>11/15) (change to thirtieths)
23. Who is the same age as Irene?	Debbie & Olivia	
24. What is the overall range of hand spans?	5cm	(22cm - 17cm)
25. What shoe size is the mode?	6	
26. Who has the same arm span as Zoe?	Megan	
27. Who has the same shoe size as Tanya?	Lorna	
28. How much older is Wendy than Debbie?	9 months	
29. How much taller is Anna than Sally?	17cm	
30. What is the overall range of height?	20cm	(174cm - 154cm)

Data Handling

No	Name	School Year	Age	Height	Arm Span	Shoe Size	Children in Family	L or R Handed	Hand Span
1	Anna	11	15y 8m	174 cm	162 cm	7	1	R	22 cm
2	Beth	11	15y 9m	168 cm	158 cm	5	2	R	21 cm
3	Carol	11	15y 0m	156 cm	162 cm	5	2	R	18 cm
4	Debbie	11	15y 7m	164 cm	166 cm	6	1	L	19 cm
5	Ellen	11	15y 8m	158 cm	159 cm	5.5	3	R	18 cm
6	Fiona	11	15y 10m	164 cm	165 cm	6	2	L	19 cm
7	Gemma	11	15y 4m	154 cm	152 cm	4	1	R	17 cm
8	Hayley	11	15y 4m	159 cm	158 cm	5	2	R	19 cm
9	Irene	11	15y 7m	170 cm	175 cm	7	4	R	20 cm
10	Jenny	11	15y 11m	169 cm	172 cm	6.5	1	L	21 cm
11	Kerry	11	15y 9m	167 cm	165 cm	5.5	2	R	21 cm
12	Lorna	11	15y 6m	156 cm	157 cm	4.5	2	R	19 cm
13	Megan	11	15y 3m	169 cm	170 cm	6	1	R	22 cm
14	Nayha	11	15y 2m	167 cm	166 cm	5	3	R	19 cm
15	Olivia	11	15y 7m	169 cm	167 cm	5.5	2	L	20 cm
16	Punimdeep	12	16y 5m	168 cm	166 cm	6	1	L	19 cm
17	Rachel	12	16y 7m	169 cm	167 cm	6	2	R	18 cm
18	Sally	12	16y 9m	157 cm	158 cm	4	6	R	17 cm
19	Tanya	12	16y 0m	162 cm	164 cm	4.5	2	R	18 cm
20	Ursula	12	16y 4m	172 cm	168 cm	7	1	L	22 cm
21	Victoria	12	16y 6m	169 cm	171 cm	6.5	2	R	20 cm
22	Wendy	12	16y 4m	166 cm	168 cm	6	3	R	21 cm
23	Xena	12	16y 2m	169 cm	167 cm	6	5	R	21 cm
24	Yvonne	12	16y 11m	164 cm	166 cm	5.5	3	R	20 cm
25	Zoe	12	16y 8m	167 cm	170 cm	6.5	1	R	22 cm

Reading Scales

This activity is a rather unusual one but offers a most useful way to practise reading different kinds of scales and estimating the values being pointed to. All six diagrams use different ranges of numbers and so there is no risk of going to the wrong one with a particular value. Each reading leads to a unique letter of the alphabet and thus to a word from the mathematical vocabulary.

What does each pupil require?
A photocopy of the diagram opposite, showing the six different kinds of scales and the readings which are required from them.
Some paper or a whiteboard to record the letters and words one by one.

What does the teacher require?
A set of suitable questions and their answers.

Procedure:
Read out the numbers and ask the pupils to write down the corresponding letters until the word is complete.

Since the words are all from the mathematical vocabulary and it would be a good idea to ask both for a definition and a sentence including the word as well as for the actual answer.

Set A Questions	Answers
1. 48, 22.4, 5.2, -6	GRAM
2. 2.62, -2, 23.8, 22.9	PLUS
3. 16.64, 32, 22.4, 2.56	ZERO
4. 22.9, 65, 48, 2.51	SIGN
5. 5.5, 65, 5.2, 22.9	BIAS
6. 32, 16.52, 5.2, 6.4, 23.3	EXACT
7. 2.62, 22.4, 2.56, 16.42, 32	PROVE
8. 22.9, 2.62, 5.2, 6.4, 32	SPACE
9. 2.62, 2.56, 65, 2.51, 23.3	POINT
10. -2, 2.56, 6.4, 23.8, 22.9	LOCUS

Set B Questions	Answers
1. -6, 65, -2, 32	MILE
2. 2.62, 65, 2.51, 23.3	PINT
3. 4, 65, -2, 2.56	KILO
4. 6.4, 23.8, 5.5, 32	CUBE
5. 40, 2.56, 23.8, 22.4	FOUR
6. 2.56, 16.42, 2.56, 65, 6.8	OVOID
7. 48, 22.4, 5.2, 2.62, 56	GRAPH
8. 2.62, 22.4, 65, -6, 32	PRIME
9. 48, -2, 2.56, 5.5, 32	GLOBE
10. 40, 2.56, 22.4, 6.4, 32	FORCE

The table below shows the scale reading corresponding to each letter of the alphabet. It can be used to construct appropriate words or phrases for your class.

Key

A = 5.2	E = 32	J = 8	N = 2.51	R = 22.4	V = 16.42
B = 5.5	F = 40	K = 4	O = 2.56	S = 22.9	W = 16.46
C = 6.4	G = 48	L = -2	P = 2.62	T = 23.3	X = 16.52
D = 6.8	H = 56	M = -6	Q = 2.67	U = 23.8	Y = 16.58
	I = 65				Z = 16.64

If more practice is needed then pupils can make up sets of words for each other. Such a project might also be suitable for an open evening or a special maths day. Different types of scales with their corresponding pointers and letters could be constructed in wood or card and hung on the walls in rooms or along a corridor.

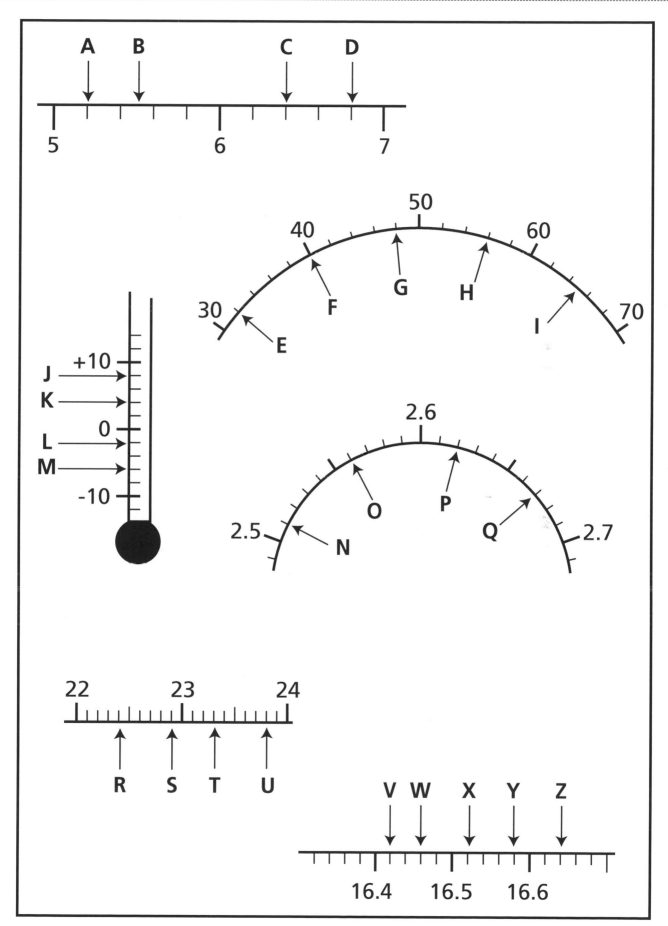

Number Machines

A number machine is a kind of imaginary black box where one number is entered into the left hand side (the input) and after being subjected to some mysterious transformation becomes another number which emerges from the right hand side (the output). In all of the examples here, each number machine has two operators, one after the other. The actions of the two operators are independent with the result of the first operation being fed into the second operator. This activity is presented in the form of four possible answers only one of which is correct Everyone can display what they think is the correct answer by holding up one of the cards showing the letters A, B, C, D, obtained from pages 7 & 8.

What does each pupil require?
A photocopy of the diagram opposite showing ten numbers machines.
A set of four cards showing A, B, C, D, ideally in different colours.

What does the teacher require?
A set of ten questions made up of a set of six pairs of operators and four pairs of input and output numbers where only one of each set is correct.

Procedure:
For the first six machines, read out the operators to be placed into the blank boxes. These operators apply to all four input numbers but only one leads to the given output number. The pupils can write them in the boxes on the sheet.

For the remaining four, read out the input and output numbers and ask them to work out which of the pair of operations is the correct one to produce the given output.

First Set of Questions

Number	Operations		
Machine 1.	x2	+2	A (3 x 2 + 2 = 8)
2.	x3	+2	C (5 x 3 + 2 = 17)
3.	x3	+7	D (3 x 3 + 7 = 16)
4.	x4	-3	B (8 x 4 - 3 = 29)
5.	-2	÷2	A ((4 - 2) ÷ 2 = 1)
6.	+4	÷3	A ((2 + 4) ÷ 3 = 2)

	In	Out	
7.	8	30	B (8 x 4 - 2 = 30)
8.	11	7	B ((11 + 3) ÷ 2 = 7)
9.	9	13	C (9 x 2 - 5 = 13)
10.	21	28	D ((21 - 7) x 2 = 28)

Second Set of Questions

Number	Operations		
Machine 1.	+3	x2	C ((2 + 3) x 2 = 10)
2.	+4	x3	B ((7 + 4) x 3 = 33)
3.	+3	x4	C ((2 + 3) x 4 = 20)
4.	-2	x4	A ((3 - 2) x 4 = 4)
5.	+7	÷3	D ((8 + 7) ÷ 3 = 5)
6.	+8	÷2	C ((20 + 8) ÷ 2 = 14)

	In	Out	
7.	4	21	C ((4 + 3) x 3 = 21)
8.	19	31	C (19 x 2 - 7 = 31)
9.	13	11	B ((13 + 9) ÷ 2 = 11)
10.	9	3	C ((9 - 3) ÷ 2 = 3)

Third Set of Questions

Number	Operations		
Machine 1.	x4	+3	D (5 x 4 + 3 = 23)
2.	+5	x2	D ((6 + 5) x 2 = 22)
3.	x3	-1	B (5 x 3 - 1 = 14)
4.	-2	x2	C ((4 - 2) x 2 = 4)
5.	÷2	+4	C (6 ÷ 2 + 4 = 7)
6.	x5	÷2	B (8 x 5 ÷ 2 = 20)

	In	Out	
7.	6	9	D (6 x 3 ÷ 2 = 9)
8.	15	4	A ((15 + 1) ÷ 4 = 4)
9.	11	8	D ((11 + 5) ÷ 2 = 8)
10.	27	15	A ((27 + 3) ÷ 2 = 15)

Fourth Set of Questions

Number	Operations		
Machine 1.	+2	x2	B ((8 + 2) x 2 = 20)
2.	x4	-1	A (4 x 4 - 1 = 15)
3.	x4	+8	A (1 x 4 + 8 = 12)
4.	-2	x3	D ((9 - 2) x 3 = 21)
5.	x3	÷5	B (10 x 3 ÷ 5 = 6)
6.	x3	÷2	D (14 x 3 ÷ 2 = 21)

	In	Out	
7.	7	3	A ((7 + 5) ÷ 4 = 3)
8.	7	4	D ((7 - 5) x 2 = 4)
9.	15	22	A ((15 - 4) x 2 = 22)
10.	15	7	B (15 ÷ 3 + 2 = 7)

There could be discussion about how you write the answers if the input is x.

Number Machines

1.

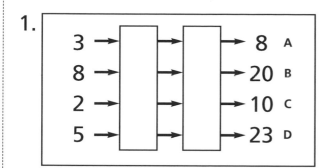

3 → →	→ 8	A
8 → →	→ 20	B
2 → →	→ 10	C
5 → →	→ 23	D

2.

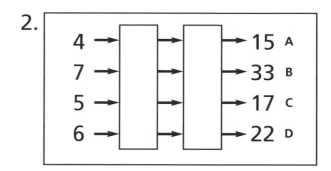

4 → →	→ 15	A
7 → →	→ 33	B
5 → →	→ 17	C
6 → →	→ 22	D

3.

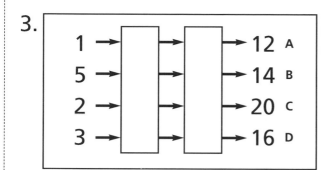

1 → →	→ 12	A
5 → →	→ 14	B
2 → →	→ 20	C
3 → →	→ 16	D

4.

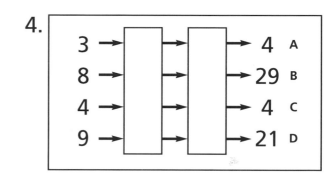

3 → →	→ 4	A
8 → →	→ 29	B
4 → →	→ 4	C
9 → →	→ 21	D

5.

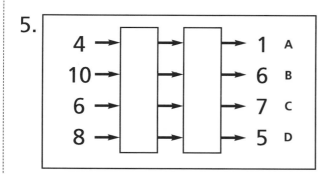

4 → →	→ 1	A
10 → →	→ 6	B
6 → →	→ 7	C
8 → →	→ 5	D

6.

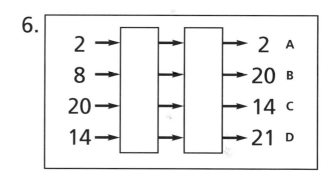

2 → →	→ 2	A
8 → →	→ 20	B
20 → →	→ 14	C
14 → →	→ 21	D

7.

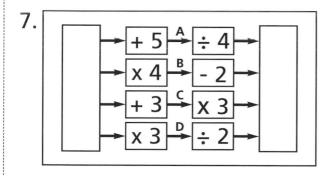

	A		
+ 5		÷ 4	
x 4	B	- 2	
+ 3	C	x 3	
x 3	D	÷ 2	

8.

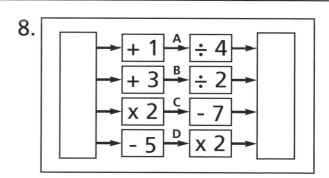

	A		
+ 1		÷ 4	
+ 3	B	÷ 2	
x 2	C	- 7	
- 5	D	x 2	

9.

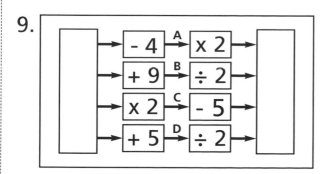

	A		
- 4		x 2	
+ 9	B	÷ 2	
x 2	C	- 5	
+ 5	D	÷ 2	

10.

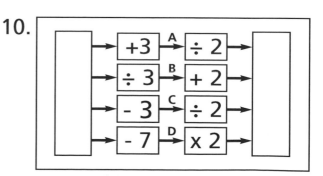

	A		
+3		÷ 2	
÷ 3	B	+ 2	
- 3	C	÷ 2	
- 7	D	x 2	

Mathematical Bluff

This activity is loosely based on the television game 'Call My Bluff' where three different definitions are given for an obscure word and the panellists have to pick out the correct meaning. In this version, the choice is between three different but similar words in a definition.

The examples given below are all to do with mathematical vocabulary but number properties or simple sums would also be suitable for a classroom activity organised in this way.

What does each pupil require?
Three cards with the letters A, B, C, preferably in different colours. Use the photocopy masters on pages 7 and 8.

What does the teacher require?
A set of definitions and the correct answers.
A list of the names of the pupils taking part.

Procedure:
The teacher reads out the three alternative definitions and then the class members hold up the letter that matches the correct answer. It is best to say something like 'now' at the end of the definitions so that all the class show their cards at the same time.

It is useful to have a list of all the names in the class and mark down just those who got it wrong. The advantage of the different colours for different answers will be apparent here.

1.
A: The point where the x and y axes meet is called the orient.
B: The point where the x and y axes meet is called the origin.
C: The point where the x and y axes meet is called the origami.

B: Origin

2.
A: The longest side of a right angled triangle is called the hippopotamus.
B: The longest side of a right angled triangle is called the hypnotist.
C: The longest side of a right angled triangle is called the hypotenuse.

C: Hypotenuse

3.
A: A polygon with eight sides is called an octagon.
B: A polygon with eight sides is called an octopus.
C: A polygon with eight sides is called an octahedron.

A: Octagon

4.
A: A whole number is called an interval.
B: A whole number is called an intercept.
C: A whole number is called an integer.

C: Integer

5.
A: A number that will divide exactly into another number is a factor.
B: A number that will divide exactly into another number is a multiple.
C: A number that will divide exactly into another number is a quotient.

A: Factor

6.
A: Another word that means the answer to a multiplication is sum.
B: Another word that means the answer to a multiplication is product.
C: Another word that means the answer to a multiplication is quotient.

B: Product

7.
A: The top number of a fraction is called the numerator.
B: The top number of a fraction is called the numeral.
C: The top number of a fraction is called the denominator.

A: Numerator

8.
A: An angle between 90° and 180° is called obese.
B: An angle between 90° and 180° is called obstinate.
C: An angle between 90° and 180° is called obtuse.

C: Obtuse

9.
A: A 4 sided shape with exactly one pair of parallel sides is called a trapeze.
B: A 4 sided shape with exactly one pair of parallel sides is called a tapestry
C: A 4 sided shape with exactly one pair of parallel sides is called a trapezium.

C: Trapezium.

10.
A: Angles between parallel lines which form a Z shape are called alternate.
B: Angles between parallel lines which form a Z shape are called corresponding.
C: Angles between parallel lines which form a Z shape are called adjacent.

A: Alternate